## Rain Forest Life

# Conservation of the Rain Forest

by Julie Murray

Dash!
LEVELED READERS
An Imprint of Abdo Zoom • abdobooks.com

# Dash!
## LEVELED READERS

### Level 1 – Beginning
Short and simple sentences with familiar words or patterns for children who are beginning to understand how letters and sounds go together.

### Level 2 – Emerging
Longer words and sentences with more complex language patterns for readers who are practicing common words and letter sounds.

### Level 3 – Transitional
More developed language and vocabulary for readers who are becoming more independent.

abdobooks.com

Published by Abdo Zoom, a division of ABDO, PO Box 398166, Minneapolis, Minnesota 55439. Copyright © 2023 by Abdo Consulting Group, Inc. International copyrights reserved in all countries. No part of this book may be reproduced in any form without written permission from the publisher. Dash!™ is a trademark and logo of Abdo Zoom.

Printed in the United States of America, North Mankato, Minnesota.
102022
012023

Photo Credits: Getty Images, Science Source, Shutterstock
Production Contributors: Kenny Abdo, Jennie Forsberg, Grace Hansen, John Hansen
Design Contributors: Candice Keimig, Neil Klinepier

Library of Congress Control Number: 2022937234

Publisher's Cataloging in Publication Data
Names: Murray, Julie, author.
Title: Conservation of the rain forest / by Julie Murray
Description: Minneapolis, Minnesota : Abdo Zoom, 2023 | Series: Rain forest life | Includes online resources and index.
Identifiers: ISBN 9781098280093 (lib. bdg.) | ISBN 9781098280628 (ebook) | ISBN 9781098280925 (Read-to-Me ebook)
Subjects: LCSH: Rain forest conservation--Juvenile literature. | Rain forests--Juvenile literature. | Temperate rain forest ecology--Juvenile literature. | Biotic communities--Juvenile literature.
Classification: DDC 577.34--dc23

# Table of Contents

Conservation of the
Rain Forest . . . . . . . . . . . . . . . . . 4

Ways to Protect the
Rain Forest . . . . . . . . . . . . . . . . 12

More Facts . . . . . . . . . . . . . . . . 22

Glossary . . . . . . . . . . . . . . . . . . 23

Index . . . . . . . . . . . . . . . . . . . . 24

Online Resources . . . . . . . . . 24

# Conservation of the Rain Forest

Rain forests are important to all life on Earth. But over the years they have slowly disappeared.

Rain forests once covered 14% of the Earth's surface. Today, they cover just 6%.

Tropical rain forest

Deforestation is one cause for the loss of rain forests. Everyday products made from trees are in high demand.

Ranching and farming are also reasons for deforestation. The trees are cut to make room for cattle and crops.

# Ways to Protect the Rain Forest

Restoration is one way humans can help rain forests. This is done by planting new trees in areas that have been cleared.

**Ecotourism** is another way to help rain forests. The money brought in can be used to protect the land.

Education is also important. Businesses and people should know how they can make a difference each day.

**Laws** can help protect rain forests. Governments need to work together to keep rain forests safe.

The loss of rain forests is devastating to people, animals, and the Earth. Saving rain forests is **crucial**!

# More Facts

- Rain forests help regulate Earth's **climate**. They also provide humans with food, medicine, and other products.

- About 200,000 acres (81,000 ha) of rain forests are lost every day.

- Scientists think rain forests could disappear in 100 years.

# Glossary

**climate** – the usual weather conditions in a place.

**crucial** – very important.

**ecotourism** – recreational travel to areas of natural or ecological interest carried out in a manner that respects the visited environment.

**law** – any one rule that government makes and that people in a society must obey.

# Index

deforestation 8, 10

education 17

farming 10

government 18

laws 18

protection 17, 18

ranching 10

range (tropical rain forest) 7

restoration 12

# Online Resources

Booklinks
NONFICTION NETWORK
FREE! ONLINE NONFICTION RESOURCES

To learn more about conserving the rain forest, please visit **abdobooklinks.com** or scan this QR code. These links are routinely monitored and updated to provide the most current information available.